POST

MW01169976

by
Carl Cook

To Michelle
Thanks for your
encouraging words
Carl
95'

Vega Press, P.O. Box 784, Sicklerville, NJ 08081

iii

Copyright © 1995 by Carl Cook
Cover photograph by Hopeton Stewart.
Cover design by Carl Cook.

Typeset in Times by Vega Studios, and printed in the United
States of America.
This a trade paperback original from Vega Press,
P.O. Box 784, Sicklerville, NJ 08081.

First edition, first printing: November, 1994

Library of Congress Cataloging-in-Publication Data

Cook , Carl , 1950-
    Postscripts / by Carl Cook. -- 1st ed.
        p.   cm.
    ISBN 1-880729-09-1
    1. Gay men--United States--Poetry. 2. Afro-American
gays--Poetry. 3. Afro-American men--Poetry. I. Title.
PS3553.055315P67   1994
811'.54--dc20   94-23596
                                                    CIP

Printed by McNaughton & Gunn Inc., 960 Woodland Drive,
Saline, Michigan 48176.

The author wishes to thank Vega Press, Michele Karlsberg,
Jason Coffman, and the late Assotto Saint for their inspira-
tion and invaluable contributions in the making of this book.

To all my loves, past and present

CONTENTS

POSTSCRIPTS

II   Let this harvest pass, o love...

III   And like a good doctor...

POSTSCRIPTS

perhaps there is something
we do not know...

Postscript #26

I

You never notice how I watch you...

Postscript #1

1

I did not get a chance
to look into
your eyes last night.
you were content

to let the moments testify
and validate the rich
full feeling of being satisfied
to have your love so near...

2

Not even sex could make
this better. the body
feels not everything. the spatial
implication of what we see

falls short of what is focused
in the heart. not even
the heart knows everything but ever
so lightly tiptoes into joy.

Postscript #2

1

I wonder if, together, we
could build a bridge
that only the two of us could
cross and not look back

to find the jackals at our heels,
trying ferociously to maul
us down, as if our deaths would
mean the end of all our kind.

2

Of course, whatever bridges we build
many others will follow. not
only of our kind but those with whom
we fought, who now look down

into the perilous rocks envisioning
their own splattered bodies
and realize, almost too late, the bridge
was built primarily for them.

Postscript #3

1

I'm looking forward to spending
an evening with you. nothing
out of the way or spectacular like
ballroom dancing or drag

queen shows. something more
subdued like dinner for two
and quiet conversation, and the chance
to see what we can see.

2

Suppose we discovered a real
connection between
the two of us like intellectual
curiosity or an aversion

to extremist politics? we might even
discover something more
fundamental like a need for creative
passion and unashamed sincerity.

Postscript #4

1

You'll be coming soon to see me.
I must warn you, however,
I'm never at ease on first dates.
I stutter. I'm clumsy, and say

things ever so silly. a glass of wine
may help but usually puts
me asleep. I'm not very good at social
graces as you can see.

2

You're different. your ways are suave
and self-assured. I should have
confidence in your coming and patience
with your charms. I know that as

the night evolves my shackles will be
unleashed, and with your low
commanding whispers, I'll enter uninhibited
the kingdom of your charms.

Postscript #5

it's good to know
there are some
like you
who do not confuse love
with the length
of their erogenous zone

and resist the fashion
to assume a date will end in bed
or verbal propositions
to get me there

and keeping
steadfast to my principles
I'd like to make an
exception

Postscript #6

1

Allow me to give you a brief history
of myself. I was born here
in Philadelphia where folks did not take
too kindly to my gayness. Mom

would have had a fit if I brought
David home to meet her. he
was cute and tough and strong, although he
needed me for other qualities.

2

That was in the eighth grade, a long time
ago. the year before that I
fell in love with my seventh grade
teacher, who never suspected.

so as you can see I was always quite
the romantic, falling in and out
of love, too reticent to approach but
always waiting with open palm.

Postscript #7

1

You never notice how I watch you
as you walk away. it's not
that I'm a voyeur, I'm not. simply
partial to posterior rhythms.

you move so innocently. I'm sure
it's deceptive though not
in a dishonest way like a cover-up
of hidden flamboyance.

2

You're so methodical in conversation, attending
to every detail, never losing your
cool, keeping balance and objectivity.
you're a master of restraint.

what would happen if I chose to speak
more personally and confessed
to you exactly what I felt. better still
would you care to slow dance?

Postscript #8

1

And maybe on the way we could
stop under an old covered
bridge in some quaint county
in West Virginia, steal a

kiss and a warm caress, what folk
in Appalachia would lynch
us for just to have some fun with
"dem faggots from duh city."

2

It's a dangerous thing to have courage.
it's safer to make fear your
companion. safer still to allow others
to think and feel and act for you.

if the wind should blow, say to yourself,
"it's only the wind. it shall pass."
then hitch a ride with your sweet ideal
and start a riot in Appalachia.

Postscript #9

1

Anything could have happened.
I was concerned. I knew
I would miss your eyes the color
of raindrops, your hairy legs,

your boyish smile. before you left
I wondered if we could date
but was too shy to ask. and needed
to know, am I too old?

2

Texas is a long way from Philadelphia.
it must be true about absence
and the heart. I'm beginning to feel it.
I was born ten years too soon.

no matter. when you return I shall
greet you as I should have
before you left, with a caring and
a tenderness I think you need.

Postscript #10

1

So often in your presence
I feel like the Baron
Munchausen, foolish and
fantastical, prepared

for the next adventure of emotional
bliss. a view into a higher
world where death is only temporary
and dreams are real.

2

Falling in love is always
for the first time,
like entering a cave again
and again, not knowing

exactly if the foot will slip
but risking it anyway
because the air is as new
as another world.

Postscript #11

1

I thought the evening unfolded
so vividly. dinner for two,
vegetarian-style, cool jazz on
the radio, splashing waters

from the fountain below. you're
an exquisite cook, baby. you
planned it so well. I was impressed,
inspired, intrigued, and enticed.

2

The movie was not as good as we
had thought. a few laughs
here and there, and that was it.
it was not the prelude

to passion we expected. but something
happened in your apartment. time
stood still. moments began to swell. I
stroked your legs, and then...

Postscript #12

1

I'm going to undress you now
since I've never seen you
naked. I imagine you thin and tight
like a tennis star, poised

to deliver the next serve,
determined, above all,
to catch me off balance
so you might score.

2

Behind those ecclesiastical manners
lie worldly desires your body
informs me of and your cool restraint
is nothing more than a harness

to hold in check your need for passion
and release. every pore and orifice
a welcomed receptacle and I shall be most
gracious to enter as your guest.

Postscript #13

1

Your windows were opened, your shades
were up, a silent breeze blew across
my brow. the room was lit with candles
as if confessions were in order.

I could see through the windows the square
down below. an old man stood
while his terrier peed. they both were like
frozen figures in a wax museum.

2

We were busy with other things. animate
with lust, lurking to attack. blest
with the passion to be so and seizing each
second as a privilege of being. in that

moment we were alive without limit,
and took advantage to awaken
the slumbering flesh. a steady kiss,
a velvet lick, the proverbial bite.

Postscript #14

I'm glad to have found you
so adaptable.
your mind not fixed
like most
but flexible
able to expand
to comprehend the subtleties
of the moment.

we need more men
like you
conflicts would be fewer
and power would not enter
into relationships.

and now
    my love
        on your knees.

Postscript #15

1

I know now it is not my body
that beguiles you. it is not
the warmth of my embrace or the slow
bear-like movements I make

approaching your desire. nor can
I say this urge to have me
in your bed or mine, alone or with
others, compels this magnetism.

2

I notice this about you, not every
kiss is physical. it's almost
like holy communion or breaking
bread with our brethren.

angels descend to guide us, carefully
knotting love with lust and
chiding us to keep it so, that we might
know God, above and below.

Postscript #16

1

I wanted to do more. my nerves
wouldn't let me. shy guys
are like that but only in the beginning.
we act a bit reserved and

conservative at first, then carefully
unwrap our fantasies,
desires, and thunderous urges
that beckon to speak.

2

We whisper things like, "Lie back
for a moment." and "Can you
feel this?" and "Yeahhh." and then,
"Right there. right there, baby."

And then the monologue ceases.
fingers like feathers are felt
in a rush, a slow oozing tongue enters
a tunnel. you scream. I cum.

Postscript #17

1

I won't have too much to say
on our next date. I'm
beginning to know you. not
so much in a private way

like knowing your habits or your
favorite drink but in a way
less mundane like destiny, if you
believe, or transcendence.

2

Of course, one would be foolish
to ignore the mystique
of your body, the impulse
to speak with hands,

legs, lip-touch and eyes, seeking
empowerment, a commission
to capture the animal, command him
on leash, and release his longing.

Postscript #18

1

It was not for lust
I brought you
to my bed. it was not
the body begging

a sharp release, a feast
of unfamiliar delights,
choosing all, tasting all
into the night.

2

You hid your essence
behind a feigned mask
spoiling the exponential light.
I peeled away the layers

intuitively felt and cast them
on a quiet shore.
this naked revelation is why
I find you here with me.

Postscript #19

I have awakened
        to find you here
    next to me

Postscript #20

1

This week alone I missed
three nights of sleep.
my need to explore fantasies
commanded my time.

you were there in every segment,
seducing the furies
of translucent lust. clearing
my head of velocities.

2

What is it about love that makes
one dream? canceling all
rest while begging for release, placing
a premium on runaway

thoughts, anticipations of celestial
cum. it won't be long before
this madness ends. I'll see you
tomorrow. my fire. my fuel.

Postscript #21

I don't know why
but spring
reminds me
so much of you

the earth renews itself
like a host
of second comings
and all the creatures
of the heavens
singing praise...

perhaps it is
the stillness in the silent grass
at night
or a million
verdurous leaves
bearing shade

it may of course
be just the shape of things
when thinking of you
my spring

Postscript #22

1

It seemed so very right in the dark
but I really needed to see
you. the lamp light illuminated
the walls in half-tones

casting you in an aura I had not
known before. your ass, so
round, so smooth, and upturned like
melons, ripe, for the market.

2

My tongue became the lance
to split them open,
hoping to taste the center,
the sweet center, firm,

and taut, and slippery. it lured me in
like echoes from a tunnel.
blindly, I touched along the walls
and felt your quivers.

Postscript #23

1

Sometimes love is temporary,
not meant to see a gray
hair ever. spared from rheumatism
and elderly malfunctions,

love in this light is anathema.
some loves pass in a day
and some in a year while others
expire on an evening's huff.

2

It remains to be seen how your love
grows, if the wink in your eye
becomes a glare in mine, if Saturday's
caress becomes tomorrow's

commitment. it's much too soon to say.
but I'm sure of this, I'll be in my
garden planting more seeds and picking
those weeds that would spoil it all.

Postscript #24

1

Sunday morning. I pray to the holy
spirit. I think of you. I know
my Lord will bless you wherever
you are, somewhere on a road

in Pennsylvania. you're getting closer
to a place where we can meet.
away from plazas of preconceptions
and avenues of hate. we're safe.

2

Some may stare and frown with disapproval.
others will throw the largest stones
along our path. a few dare gather in the night
like mad dogs in a southern sun, looking

for retribution of their ignorance. the angels
will protect us even if our blood
is spilled and love's survival must prove
again this love was meant to be.

II

Let this harvest pass, o love...

Postscript #25

1

Let this harvest pass, o love.
not every crop can yield
expected satisfaction. the best
of weathers may take

a sudden turn, destroying
nutrients we waited
long through wintry nights
to bless our table.

2

Let this harvest pass, o Lord.
disease, distress, despair,
exempts us from living immortally,
assigning what burdens we bear

a perennial rest. this spring that once
was ours depletes the soil, turns
our little seeds into the mud now heavy,
now hushed, now heartfelt like death.

Postscript #26

perhaps there is something
we do not know
untold to us
unseen in dreams
the lyrics sung above our dreams

Postscript #27

Something so simple
as a kiss
could kill for
lack of it

or build eternal
structures
for generations
to flourish

Postscript #28

try the door
      turn the knob
ring the bell
      if you must

but under the mat
      lies the key that someone
left for you
      to make yourself at home

Postscript #29

let's walk to the beach
where the bonfire
burns and heap all our
trinkets and garbage and trash
into the great flames

Postscript #30

1

Our world is full of banalities.
moments of inconsequence.
irrational unrealities. time is
spent waiting and waiting,

for what exactly we are not sure.
a little laughter breaks
the sequence of desperation. love
is a cure for some things.

2

Come to me in the space
I have cleared for you.
seduce the furies. release the pain.
forgive the unspeakable past.

to heal is all we can hope for.
love comes easiest
with health. our hearts are seeking
a common center.

Postscript #31

1

We are whatever we are
and whatever we
deem so possible. we
tread on discovery

at every moment but only
to triumph when we
dare to dance an unsavory
waltz with defeat.

2

Not every conduit is lit
nor every promise
fulfilled. even love, at times,
retreats in desperation.

what seeds to sow and how
to sow them can yield
a harvest or a sorrow. be glad
for every fruit however small.

Postscript #32

    1

After the rain
after the streets have dried
after the drops
have fallen and ceased to dance

o where are you now?
what are your thoughts?
how will you travel
the dry terrain of naked choice?

    2

Before the sun
before the light releases you
before the shadows
disappear and find us mute...

o when to speak?
why the stammered words?
who amidst this fury
will gather our deliverance?

Postscript #33

Of death
remember this
it is not the end
of all things

merely the end
of some things and
of those things

they are not
the things eternal.

Postscript #34

1

For the memories ungranted
for the tears that could not hold torrential tides
for the hopes unheeded from
the times we failed to press the passing time

It is a coming and a coming back again
perhaps in styles and forms
we have not dared to wish
like lilacs in the wind that may be us

2

Igloos aren't the most comfortable
homes in the world but they
are adaptable and whether we like it
or not (ask any Eskimo)

we have no choice or will. living
upon glaciers thicker than
the eye can fathom requires a certain
degree of pragmatic accommodation.

Postscript #35

1

Sweet is the night air
when all lay dying.
solemn is the cricket
of a soldier's winter.

the fog rolls proverbial
across mounted
stones announcing another
name of remembrance.

2

My mother is there in her
silent way, complacent
where it is proper to be so,
prepared and waiting

for signs of redemption. so sweet
is the night air. so still
the limbs that bare no leaves.
death is a quiet wakening.

Postscript #36

when all this is over
as all this must
we may again embrace
with a tenderness
beyond this time
beyond these tears
and vain regrets

time surely cannot give us
back the years
nor reclaim the yearnings
of our youth

but the faith to forgive
the strength to redeem friendships
where we thought
we had none

and the courage
to create ourselves
anew

all this and more
we have fought
and won

III

And like a good doctor...

Postscript #37

1

You drove across disjointed highways
to see me, all the way
from Chicago in your blue Chevy Blazer
in weather too beautiful

for pictures. the kids were awake
hoping to meet this "friend"
from Illinois. my love had a smile
on his face but was suspicious.

2

We agreed to meet for dinner.
buffalo wings, salad,
fried shrimp and pasta. you were
hungry that night for food

and for love. dessert was just as good.
chocolate cake and tea, cheese cake
and coffee. hungry for food and for love.
I treated you to both.

Postscript #38

1

And like a good doctor
you carefully applied
the prophylactics, attempting
to save both our lives

during a moment when thinking
was quite difficult
and both our hearts were
set on an easy lay.

2

I fell in love just as I came.
I knew it was you
who would restore my life,
an angel of transfiguration;

a warrior armed to destroy the myth
that men like us are too crippled
to love, too preoccupied with images
to know what's good for us.

Postscript #39

1

Sin is never a graceful thing.
an ill-cure for comfort.
a sorrowful resolution to
to ambivalent feelings.

it stinks. it creates unhealthy
hesitations. it wilts
the rose and fabricates excuses
for all our stumblings.

2

Have mercy. I crawl for forgiveness.
my petals are singed like
the May dogwood. the meadows
meander and continue to bloom.

if you must, turn your naked back
and cancel our difficult
struggles together but never, never
never stop loving me.

Postscript #40

1

There was confusion, guilt,
and lust but lust
that did not last into
the night. a wet

voracious tongue explored
methodically and moved
across my lips with warm
intent and worship.

2

Our voices spoke imperatively
low. we dared not wake
the slumbering lover fearing
mistrust and certain

misunderstanding. I'm not quite
sure now if I trust myself
or have thought long enough
to understand this tryst.

Postscript #41

1

It's always nice making love
to you on the sofa down-
stairs. it's almost like a dare
that someone should ring

the doorbell and peep through
the blinds to see if we're
home only to find us humping
in the living room.

2

People are always wondering
what gays really do, who
sucks what and who fucks whom.
I suppose one day they'll

finally catch us, my love, you
on your head with your
legs outstretched, me with my long
tongue inside your ass.

Postscript #42

1

What we crave in love
is often illusive.
when asked, "why do you love him?"
we choke to answer.

then do so with clichés
or repeat the echoes
we hear from momma's grave
but seem never too sure.

2

A few silly love verses
will not suffice.
love is too complex.
we need Freud and

every other cosmic theory
just to explain it.
of course, we need not ponder
at all so long as we do it.

Postscript #43

1

My lover lies here beside me.
does he dream of me
as he snores? or just needs
rest like any good

partner. the kids made him
work today. chicken
pox the culprit. there'll be
no sex tonight. damn.

2

Marriage changes all. if you don't
think so you're not married.
it's not that we see differently
but see so much more.

And if we're honest and unafraid
so much more of ourselves.
this and a little sex to ease the night
makes it all worth it...

Postscript #44

some people think
I'm this
when I'm really that

soft-spoken
mild-mannered
a bit shy
and demure

nothing more
than a masquerade
on an afternoon

but when
the moon ascends...

Postscript #45

1

A critic once noted, the tense
in my love letters
are often confused
and convoluted,

inconsistent and somewhat
out of sync with real
time: the past, the present, the future,
hopelessly entangled.

2

I can't remember exactly
when first I kissed you.
I don't remember how we
came to share a certain

bed in a certain room
on a certain night.
I know only that the wetness
of your lips still lingers.

Postscript #46

1

No where else have I seen
such beauty. mysterious
vapors creeping across low lying
grasses, a sun too large

for the earth and bent on
blinding the retina
as if she had known we were
peeping at her petticoats.

2

"October journeys are safest,"
says Margaret, which
is why I have traveled
along uncertain rails,

endured the unexpected terrain,
the overgrowth too dense
to build a home but lush enough
to meditate on you.

Postscript #47

1

Pleasure is so becoming of you.
your body pulls me in.
I need only whisper a prayer and
you are there with an answer.

you never turn me away
to cackle with the buzzards.
you never make me feel
I am one among many.

2

Passion belongs to the living.
we mustn't forsake it.
even the vigilant owl in his
black forest will hoot

until his final hour, knowing
well some unsuspecting
mouse will skitter and tease
across his path to be taken.

Postscript #48

uhmmm... what have we here
in the tight white jeans?
fluorescent dreams
or hospital beds?
a night to cherish
or another nightmare?

I pass.
my love is waiting...

IV

Decisions will have to be made...

Postscript #49

1

Dysfunctional folk are difficult
to love whomever they are.
sons or lovers, mothers or fathers,
it matters not. distorted

interiors brimming with jagged
subconscious emotions,
looking for someone to cut to complete
their mosaic of madness.

2

I've come to love you in spite of all.
I've learned to kiss
your reluctant lips and settle reluctantly
for bimonthly sex,

although my needs are so much more.
not more, however, than you
care to give but more than you
ever dare to give.

Postscript #50

1

Like so many of us, you adored
Judy Garland, Diana Ross,
and Patti Labelle. Hollywood
theatrics and a fake sense

of elegance dressed your inner
persona with identity
as if to validate this queer
kind of manhood.

2

A deeper sense of who we are
is what we need
and the courage to fight back,
raise all kinds of hell

like the lowly ought, and forget
about all those glamour
girls who never assisted our
arduous struggles anyway.

Postscript #51

1

Decisions will have to be made.
ambiguous leanings, cover-
ups, and tell-tale signs of a messy past
will have to be filed and locked away.

engines that roar and cars much
faster than we care to drive
may slip into our personal resume
designed to impact an interview.

2

There is a threshold that cools
the thirst for living,
absorbs the sweat and leaves
the limbs relaxed.

this threshold belongs to you.
your lot has been reserved.
I stand awaiting with open palm.
your ticket is your heart.

Postscript #52

1

You accuse me again of knowing
too much and speaking
in terms you cannot grasp. for this,
I beg forgiveness.

I know nothing and never will.
the bit of knowledge I think
I know will crumble much sooner
than the crumbling earth.

2

Love has no need of academics
or metaphors too complex
to comprehend or cryptograms
too puzzling for cryptics

and mystics who have not learned
to live. what fool would
trade a dissertation for loving
you forevermore?

Postscript #53

1

I'm not putting up with your
bullshit so get use to it,
dear. masses of eternal fools
walk collectively past my

door. do not enter if it is
they you seek. behind
my door lay the infinite silence
of roses, gently, gently picked.

2

No one can ever perfectly
offer himself in love.
there is a weed somewhere
in everyone's garden.

even I sometimes forget to say
please, approaching with
molten lips on fire and not
o not to be denied.

Postscript #54

1

You may have thought I was
trying to hurt you
and misconstrued my need for
clarity as vindictiveness

or just plain bitchiness. but
you're mistaken.
my sentiments are never daggers.
I thought you knew me better.

2

I loved you too much
and that was my error.
when you give your heart
wholly it's never

appreciated. kindness mistaken
for weakness. an open door
begins to revolve and sincerity
is shuffled from the table.

Postscript #55

1

I'll make no secret of this:
your bitchiness disturbs
me. your casual inexcusable ways
of saying things like "fuck you."

And all I wanted was quiet
sensuality, tenderness
and touches like the wisp
of a summer wind.

2

It's hard to speak of love in such
a context with you,
difficult to set the tone when power
is at the heart of things.

At any rate, your love-making
has no finesse. what more
could I expect from one whose
attitude is "fuck you?"

Postscript #56

1

Together again, there is time
for a smooth embrace.
we need each other without
the angry lips of shame.

a reconciliation
of vain presumptuous
intents which favors
nothing essential.

2

Allow me to extend my hand
and kiss the lips
that brought the lonely heart
a little closer to the stars,

straddling the dangerous
atmosphere, observing
the fiery meteors burn
into nothingness.

Postscript #57

1

I love the stillness
of a silent home,
the hush in hearing
when the children

have gone to bed and the day
can review itself,
release itself from the hustle
of morning air.

2

Tension between lovers begins
in tenderness, a calm
more certain than a country lake
which doesn't stir at all

until storm clouds descend
and move into the city
where first I met you, where
lightning first struck.

Postscript #58

nothing
memorable by way of love
no silver kisses in a tempest's nest
no resurrections from the wilted nights
where sparrows wing
across the emptiness

it was surely not
the dawning of a dream conceived
in childhood fantasies

reality heightened
(or so it seemed) to a pitch
of haze

a touch
and a touching
unspoiled by despair
of consumptive
hours

what it was
was the wakening
of morning-
glories

Postscript #59

1

I don't feel very comfortable
in this relationship
anymore. in fact, my feelings are
downright scathed.

where my heart once fluttered
it now palpitates.
I could drop dead at any moment
just thinking about it.

2

A little time for truth
is always left. we
could pretend that all is well
and ignore the goblins

at our door, continue to stumble
into a future without intent.
or simply realize it's painful to stop
loving someone you truly love.

Postscript #60

1

Wouldn't it be absurd
if there really were
a boogeyman? if every
scream in the night

meant intractable death? or every
dog who barked sunk
his teeth in another? how could
we live or ever hope to?

2

A good captain must navigate
irascible clouds, perversive
winds, invidious rocks. he knows
the steady harbor is not

too far. though every sign
and signal would turn
him back, he wants to go home.
he needs to be loved.

ABOUT THE AUTHOR

Carl Cook is a poet, teacher, and folk-artist. His first book, "The Tranquil Lake of Love," was acclaimed nationally and a finalist for the Lambda Literary Award for best Gay Men's Poetry of 1993. He continues to write, paint, and teach in Philadelphia, Pennsylvania.

All inquiries, letters, and permission requests should be sent to the author, c/o VEGA PRESS, P.O. Box 784, Sicklerville, NJ 08081.